Ellen Anderson
Feb 2000.

Three-Dimensional Flowers

in Ribbon and Fabric

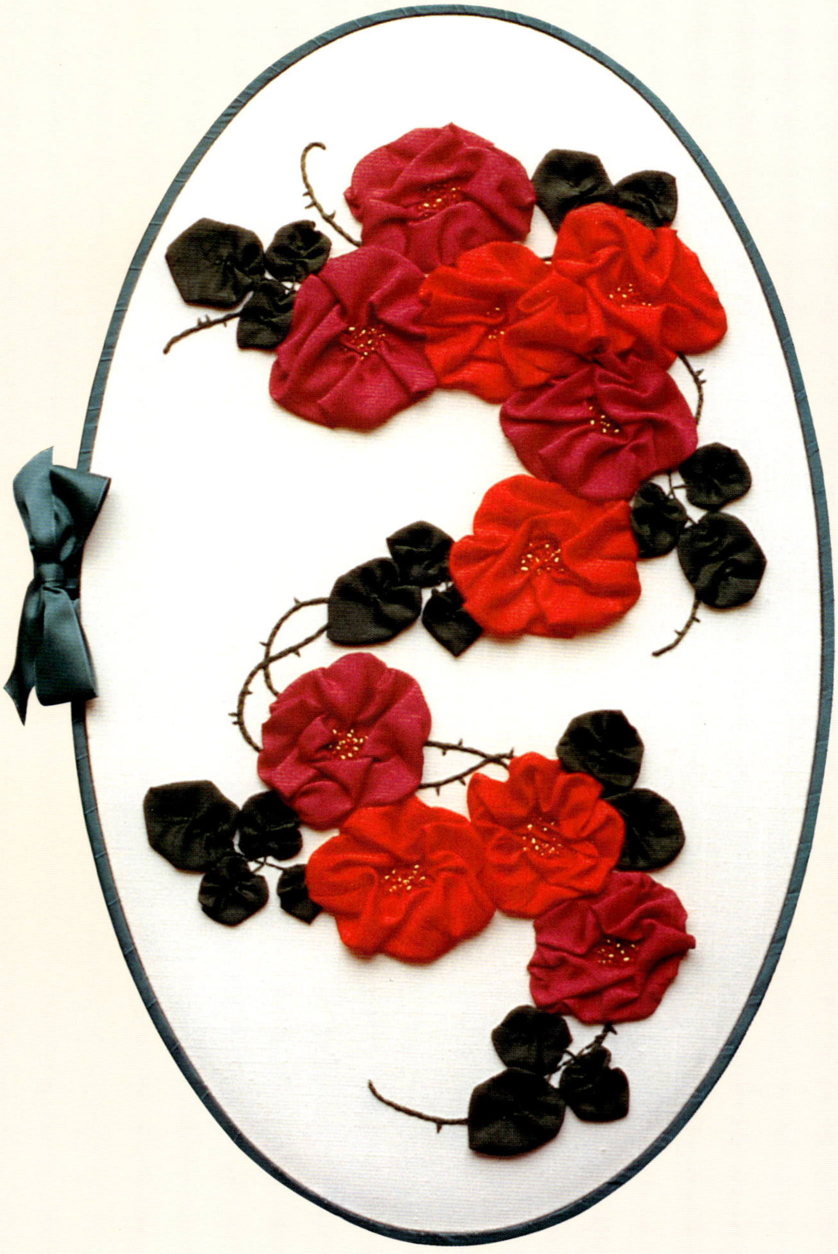

Three-Dimensional Flowers

in Ribbon and Fabric

Joyce Randall

Kangaroo Press

Frontispiece: *Red roses* (page 33)

© Joyce Randall 1997

First published in 1997 by Kangaroo Press Pty Ltd
3 Whitehall Road Kenthurst NSW 2156 Australia
PO Box 6125 Dural Delivery Centre NSW 2158
Printed in Hong Kong through Colorcraft Ltd

ISBN 0 86417 824 7

Contents

Introduction   7
Materials and techniques   8
- Frames ● Background fabrics ● Ribbons
- Furnishing fabric ● Beads ● Transferring designs
- Making up you own designs ● Ribbon embroidery techniques ● Stitches ● Folded roses
- Padding and framing

THE DESIGNS   15
Red poppies   17
Anemones   21
Bowl of chrysanthemums   23
Climbing roses   27
Apple blossom hibiscus   29
Red roses   33
Pink roses   37
Pink and purple chrysanthemums   39
Large rose plaque   42
Sunflowers   45
Pink, white and blue flowers   48
Daisy plaque   53
Yellow folded roses with violets   57
Pink single roses   58
Small mauve ribbon roses   59
Doll's hat with braided ribbon and ribbon
    roses   60
Round box with braided ribbon and ribbon
    roses   61

Detail from Pink, white and blue flowers (page 48)

Introduction

Simple, exciting and lots of fun

That one form of art can lead to an interest in many others has been proved again and again. Being a china painter for forty years has led me to the study of oil painting and acrylics and to dabbling in tapestry design and other arts and crafts, leading eventually to ribbon embroidery, beading, bonding and painting on fabric.

Flowers are one of the never-ending sources of inspiration for visual artists. Their myriad shapes and colours inspire spontaneous, exciting and original ideas; and different techniques spring to mind to accommodate them. It was a bunch of red poppies which first gave me the idea for a three-dimensional way to work with ribbon. I put them on a cream background with striking results and from then on there was no stopping me. I found ideas everywhere for this new kind of decorative floral work.

The stiffness and firmness of good nylon taffeta ribbon, and the fact that it resists fraying, and can be threaded through a chenille needle for embroidery, make it an obvious favourite to work with. Crinkled polyester dress fabric also has firmness and is soft and useful in many ways. It makes a good background material and has been used to mould some of the roses in this book.

As my designs grew in size, I found myself turning to fabrics as well as ribbon to achieve the effect I wanted. The flowers in the plaques on pages 42, 48 and 53 are worked in a suede-coated polyester and cotton curtain fabric which can be manipulated to stand well away from the background.

Bonding and beading have been used in some designs, and there are a few small silk and satin ribbon embroidered pieces given dimension with folded ribbon roses. A small straw box and doll's hat decorated with braided ribbon and folded roses are unusual inclusions.

All projects are illustrated in colour and are accompanied by pattern outlines. Note that many of the designs are quite large and have had to be reduced to fit in the book. The percentage for enlargement is given wherever necessary.

These design outlines are merely to get you started. There is endless scope for flair and originality in this three-dimensional work—please let your imagination loose.

Joyce Randall

Materials and techniques

Frames

Wooden embroidery hoops make attractive frames for this kind of work. Some quite large round and oval hoops are available. Three of the pieces in the book were done on ovals measuring 52 cm × 32 cm (20½" × 12½"). These larger hoops have special blocks attached for the screws. The blocks are rather large. It is possible, with care, to drill screw-holes closer to the frame and saw a slice off the blocks to make them less obvious. Cover the blocks by glueing ribbon over them and covering with a bow when the piece is finished. Firm satin ribbon gives the best result. It can be used for binding the frames as well, but this is not absolutely necessary as the wood looks quite attractive with only a bow to cover the screw.

The smaller plastic frames are easy to use but avoid taking the fabric out of the frame for any reason as you may have difficulty replacing it in exactly the same position.

Background fabrics

Crinkled polyester or fine imitation linen dress fabric, which both come in a variety of colours, are my preference, placed over lawn, but experiment with others for variety. A sheer material such as voile or georgette used over a strong background colour can soften the colour and give a shimmery effect. Do not use stretch fabrics because a broken or cut thread can cause the material to unravel.

Ribbons

There are different qualities and thicknesses in satin and taffeta ribbon. Always choose the stiffest and firmest for three-dimensional work. Variegated silk ribbon is a little hard to find but two or more similar colours can be substituted where the pattern calls for it. Ribbon with a fine wire along each edge, as is used in the apple blossom hibiscus design, is readily available now and is good for keeping petals and leaves in desired positions.

Furnishing fabric

Some of the designs are worked in a suede-coated polyester and cotton furnishing fabric which can be manipulated to stand well away from the background. This fabric is firm and easy to work with, does not fray, and is easy to mark on the wrong side and cut out.

Beads

Most of the beads called for in these designs are small—seed bead size or slightly larger. Leaving a small space between beads makes the work look more delicate. I prefer to use quilting needles for beading as they are firm, short and yet quite fine.

Transferring designs

As many of the designs have had to be reduced to fit in the book, always check whether the design needs to be enlarged (photocopying is easiest) before you begin tracing. Only the one enlargement is used (133%), which translates to 3 cm = 4 cm (¾" = 1") if you have to use the grid method.

To transfer a traced design to the fabric, pin the design in place using lace pins, which are very fine and less likely to leave tiny holes in fabric. Pin a piece of graphite paper (obtainable at art shops), shiny side down, between design and fabric and pin in place also to prevent it rubbing on the fabric. Use a fine-pointed ball-point pen to go over the design. This is best done on a hard surface. Use white graphite paper on coloured fabric.

Alternatively, trace the design onto paper, then pierce holes in the paper with a stiletto or wooden skewer at points such as the centres of main flowers, petal or leaf tips. Using a fade-out pen, mark these points on the fabric through the holes. Use a white pencil on coloured fabrics. Remember fade-out pen marks may fade in an hour or so.

If you are using a wooden frame and need to do some background painting, tracing or bonding before tracing on the design, place the fabric in the frame for a short time first to make a creased circular mark which will help position the preparatory work.

When tracing a design on to your work, trace inside the outlines of shapes which are to be covered by bonding or ribbon. This lessens the risk of lines showing. Mark in the centres only of some large flowers, especially cupped ones.

Making up your own designs

If you want to make up your own floral design follow a similar procedure. Mark the positions of three main flowers, usually the largest, and complete these first, as often they take up more room than expected. Using the fade-out pen try marking in secondary flowers and when you are satisfied work these too. Do the same with leaves, and then mark in stems to make the design flow. To fill out the design, use French knots to represent tiny flowers. Remember that uneven numbers of flowers usually look better.

Ribbon embroidery techniques

Silk ribbon
When working with silk ribbon, use pieces no longer than 25 cm (10"), as the ribbon can fray at the edges before a longer length is used up. Pulling the ribbon through the material slowly helps prevent fraying. Keep ribbon flat.

Needles
- For use with small beads—quilting needles (No. 10).
- For embroidery cotton or silk—crewel needles.
- For ribbon embroidery—chenille needles—fine for silk ribbon, thicker for satin and wider nylon.

Threading the needle
Cut across the end of the ribbon diagonally before threading it. Push the pointed tip of the ribbon through the eye of the needle and pull about 2 cm ($^3/_4$") through. Then push the point of the needle back through the ribbon, about 5 mm ($^3/_{16}$") from the pointed tip. Pull the ribbon back through the needle so that not much more than the tip of the ribbon is left attached. This presents less bulk when pulling the ribbon through the fabric.

Thicker or wider ribbon
If you are using satin ribbon or wide nylon ribbon it is of great importance to lessen the obstruction caused when the ribbon reaches the hole in the fabric. To help overcome this push the point of the needle back through the ribbon 5 mm ($^3/_{16}$") from the tip and close to the selvedge. The ribbon is stronger there. Pull the ribbon back through the needle and twist it backwards and forwards so that not much more than the tip of the ribbon is left attached. This again presents less bulk when pulling the ribbon through the fabric.

Use a stiletto to gently enlarge the hole if necessary. I find pliers handy sometimes to pull the needle through but I use them only if I think the fabric can take it and when the bulk of the ribbon has been minimised as far as possible.

Starting off
When starting off leave 15 or 20 mm ($^1/_2$"–$^3/_4$") of ribbon at the back of the work. If fine silk or rayon ribbon is being used, the next stitch through to the back will often pierce the starting-off end and save finishing off. Do not do this with thicker ribbon as it does not pass through itself easily. Leave it hanging at the back to be sewn down later.

Finishing off
Take the ribbon through to the back and cut it about 1 cm ($^3/_8$") from the work. You will probably have several cut-off pieces which will all need securing with needle and thread to stitches at the back of the embroidery. It is nearly impossible to keep the back of the work tidy.

Threading the needle: the needles on the left show diagonally cut nylon taffeta, satin and silk ribbons with point threaded through needle and needle taken back through the ribbon near the tip; the needles on the right are ready for sewing

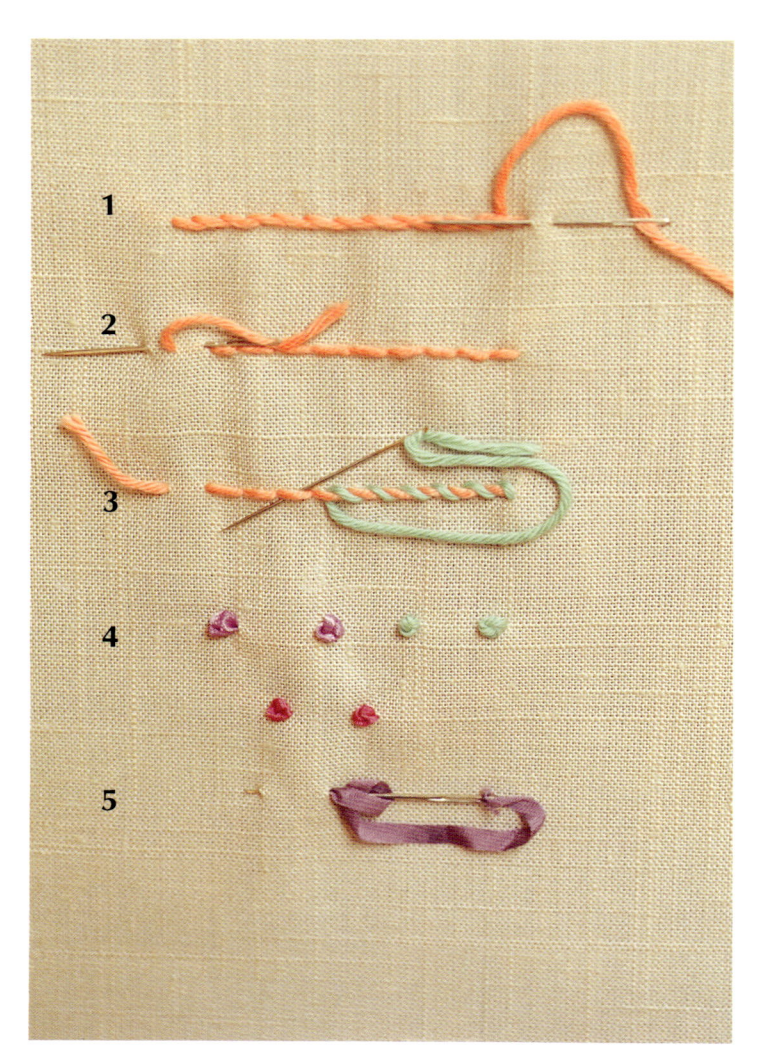

Stitches

Much floral work can be accomplished using plain straight stitches. Embroider most stems in stem stitch; backstitch can be used for an attractive alternative. For a thicker stem these stitches can be 'whipped' by sewing a thread through each stitch afterwards. French knots are useful as small flowers to fill out a design. Fly stitch can also be used for this purpose and is good as a starting point when embroidering folded (ribbon) roses.

LEFT:
1. Stem stitch
2. Back stitch
3. Whipping
4. French knots
5. Making a French knot

BELOW:
1. Making spokes of a wheel by starting with fly stitch
2. Bringing ribbon up next to centre and over and under spokes until spokes cannot be seen
3. Finished rose
4. Fly stitch—different ways

Folded roses

Folded roses can be used in designs for really pretty floral effect. A firm 7 mm (¼") satin ribbon is the best choice.

Take a length of ribbon and hold it vertically; about 14 cm (5½") up fold over horizontally to the right. Holding with the thumb, bring the short end up vertically, followed by the long end across to the left. Bring the short end down and the long end across to the right, and so on, until the short end is used up. Hold the end firmly with the thumb and first finger against the long piece of ribbon and let the folded part go. Still holding on, pull the long ribbon back carefully until the rose forms. Secure with a stitch down the middle and at the base. Trim ends and sew onto the design.

Steps in making a folded rose

Padding and framing

It is a good idea before starting any piece to place the inside hoop over a piece of stiff cardboard and run a pencil mark around the inside. Cut the cardboard out and use this later to hold in the padding. Carton cardboard makes a good backing for large pieces.

As well as the cardboard you will need:

- A piece of plastic foam the same size, varying from about 8 mm (⁵⁄₁₆") thick for plastic frames to about 20 mm (¾") for large ovals
- Roll of cotton wool
- White lawn for unlined small plastic frames to mask the colour of the plastic
- A piece of felt to cover the back, the size of outer frame.

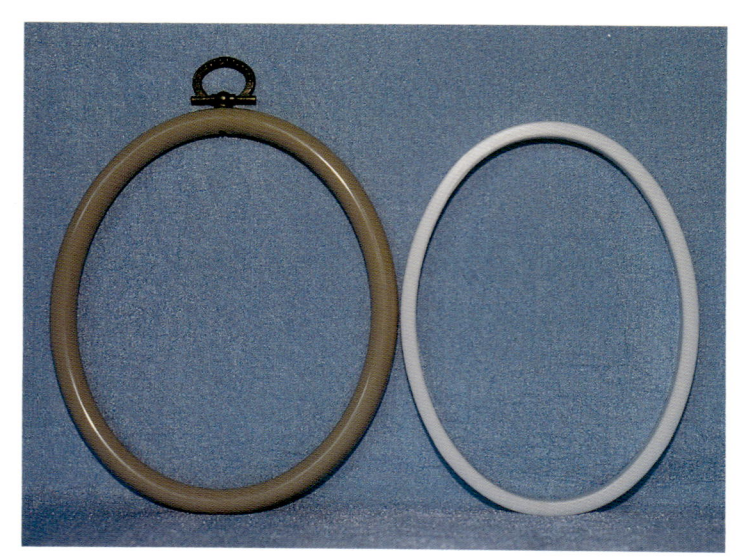

Plastic frame and insert

Lacing back of embroidery

Trim the fabric at the back leaving at least 4 cm (1½") all around for a tiny frame and at least 6 cm (2½") for a large wooden frame. Run a double thread of sewing cotton for small frames (a double thread of strong crochet cotton for large frames) around the edge of the fabric about 2 cm (¾") in from the raw edge, but do not finish off. Put the plastic foam layer next, then a smooth layer of cotton wool, thicker in the centre, followed by the cardboard.

Hold the cardboard down while tightly drawing in the gathering thread around the raw edge of the fabric. Use two or three stitches to finish off the gathering thread. Thread the needle again with a double thread and zigzag across the back, working from side to side and end to end, pulling tightly as you go. Pull tightly again before finishing off. Check that the cardboard is positioned as far as possible level with the insert. It may be necessary to go around with another thread to tighten further.

If you are using a wooden frame which is to be bound, loosen the screw at this stage and take out the centre. Bind the frame with 15–23 mm (⅝"–1") ribbon, starting at the screw and overlapping ribbon at each turn. Use a small dab of craft glue to hold in place at beginning and end. Return to frame and tighten screw well, using pliers if necessary.

To finish, cut a piece of felt the same size as the frame and attach with craft glue around edge.

Tie a ribbon bow over the screw of the wooden frame.

Lacing back of large oval frame

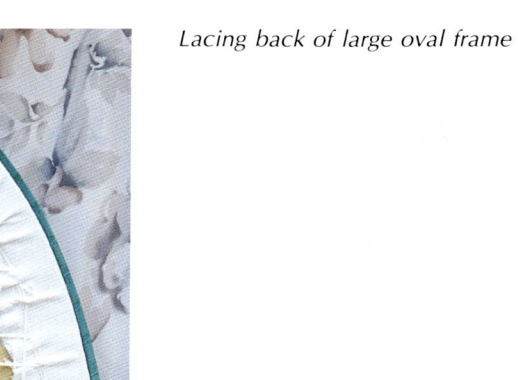

Lacing back of large rectangular plaque

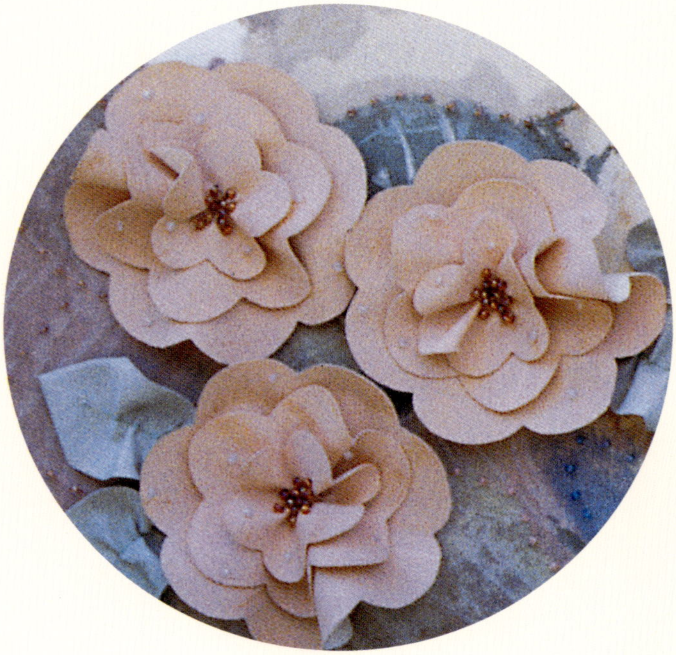

THE DESIGNS

The red poppies which began it all . . .

Red poppies

Frame 32 cm (12½") wooden embroidery hoop
Fabric Cream linen or other suitable fabric (wool-look thick polyester curtain fabric was used for this) cut at least 6 cm (2¼") larger all around than frame
  White lawn the same size for lining
Ribbon 25 mm (1") red taffeta
  3 mm green satin
  25 mm (1") green satin
Beads Tiny black beads

Place both fabrics in frame together and screw tight. Leave for a short time to crease the fabric, then unscrew and remove fabric from frame. Make pencil marks at top, bottom and sides 3 cm (1¼") outside circle. Trace on enlarged design, being careful to place in correct position, but only mark in the centres of the flowers. If using a thick fabric, make holes in the paper first with a stiletto. Make two or three holes along each stem and one where each flower centre is to be, one at each end of the leaves and to indicate bud tips. Pin design in position on the fabric and use a pencil to make a mark through each hole. Return the fabric to the frame and tighten the screw.

Start with one stem. Using a fade-out pen make a curved line to join pencil marks and pin a length of narrow green ribbon along the line. Catch down at intervals along the edges, using tiny stitches. Repeat this process for each stem.

To make the flowers, thread red ribbon through a large chenille needle. Bring through fabric from the back at the base of a petal, leaving about 2 cm (¾") on wrong side. Fold ribbon back on right side, allowing it to cup, then cut off in scalloped fashion about 4 cm (1½") from the base of the petal. Repeat this for each petal, starting them as close together in the centre as possible.

For profile flowers bring ribbon through from back and cut as for others, fold down as shown and catch in place with tiny stitches. Use tiny stitches to keep the lower petals of the other two flowers in place. Small pieces of cotton wool can be tucked under the profile flowers to add to their rounded appearance.

Pieces of 25 mm (1") green satin ribbon are used for the buds. Turn edges under and slip stitch in place over a small piece of red ribbon.

Detail of tucked petal and profile flower

Cut leaves out of the wide green satin ribbon and buttonhole in place.

Large fly stitches in green silk thread can suggest grasses. Make green knobs in flower centres using double thread of green silk or double length of green stranded cotton to make bulky French knots. Surround with black beads which, sewn on petal bases, help to keep the ribbon in a cupped position.

Tighten fabric in frame, tighten screw, pad the back and finish as shown on page 12, then loosen screw and remove embroidery from outer frame. Bind the frame with 25 mm (1") green satin ribbon, using craft glue to secure ends. Return embroidery to hoop, tighten screw well and cover with bow. Attach felt backing with craft glue around edge.

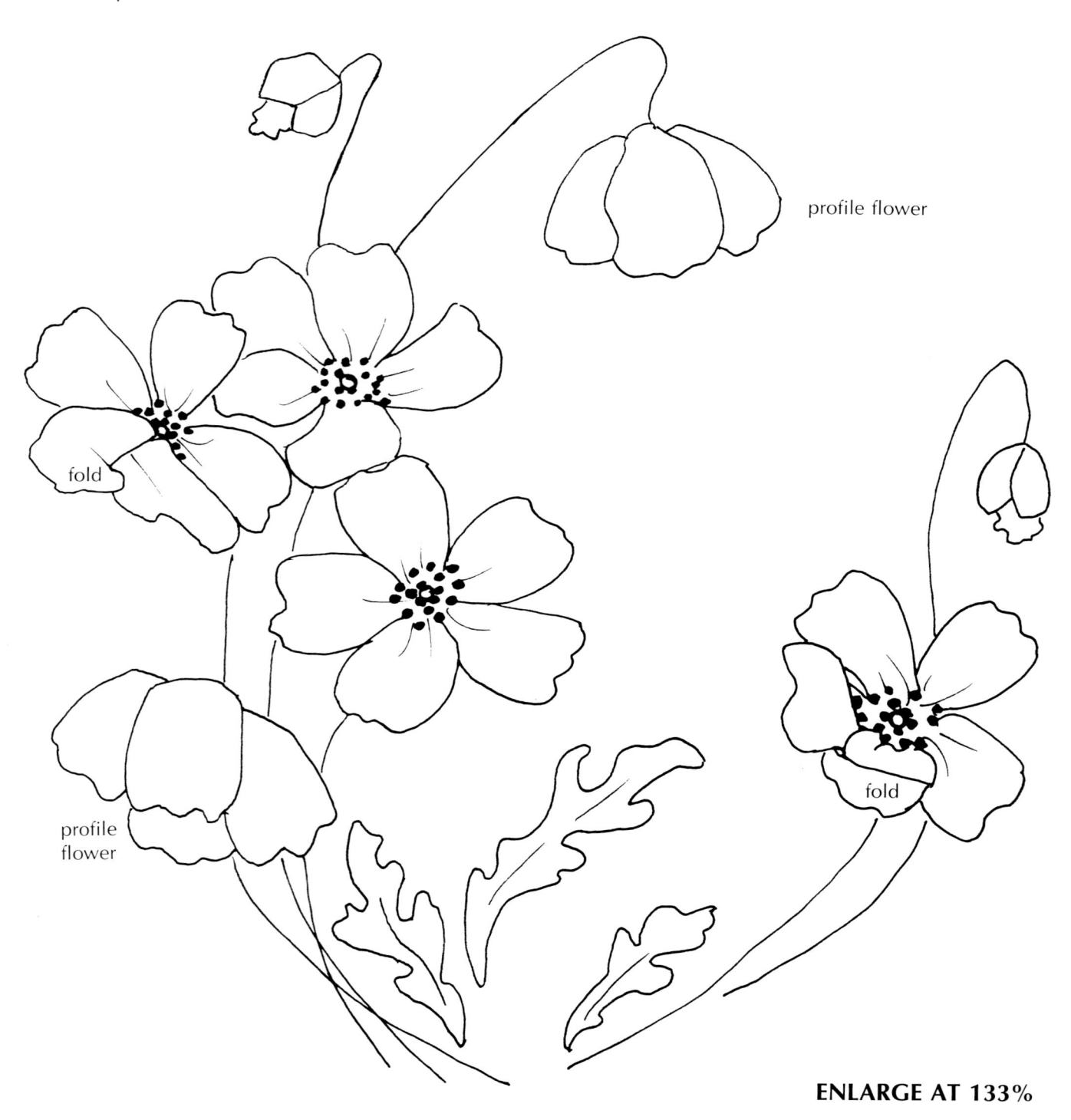

profile flower

fold

profile flower

fold

ENLARGE AT 133%

Anemones (page 21)

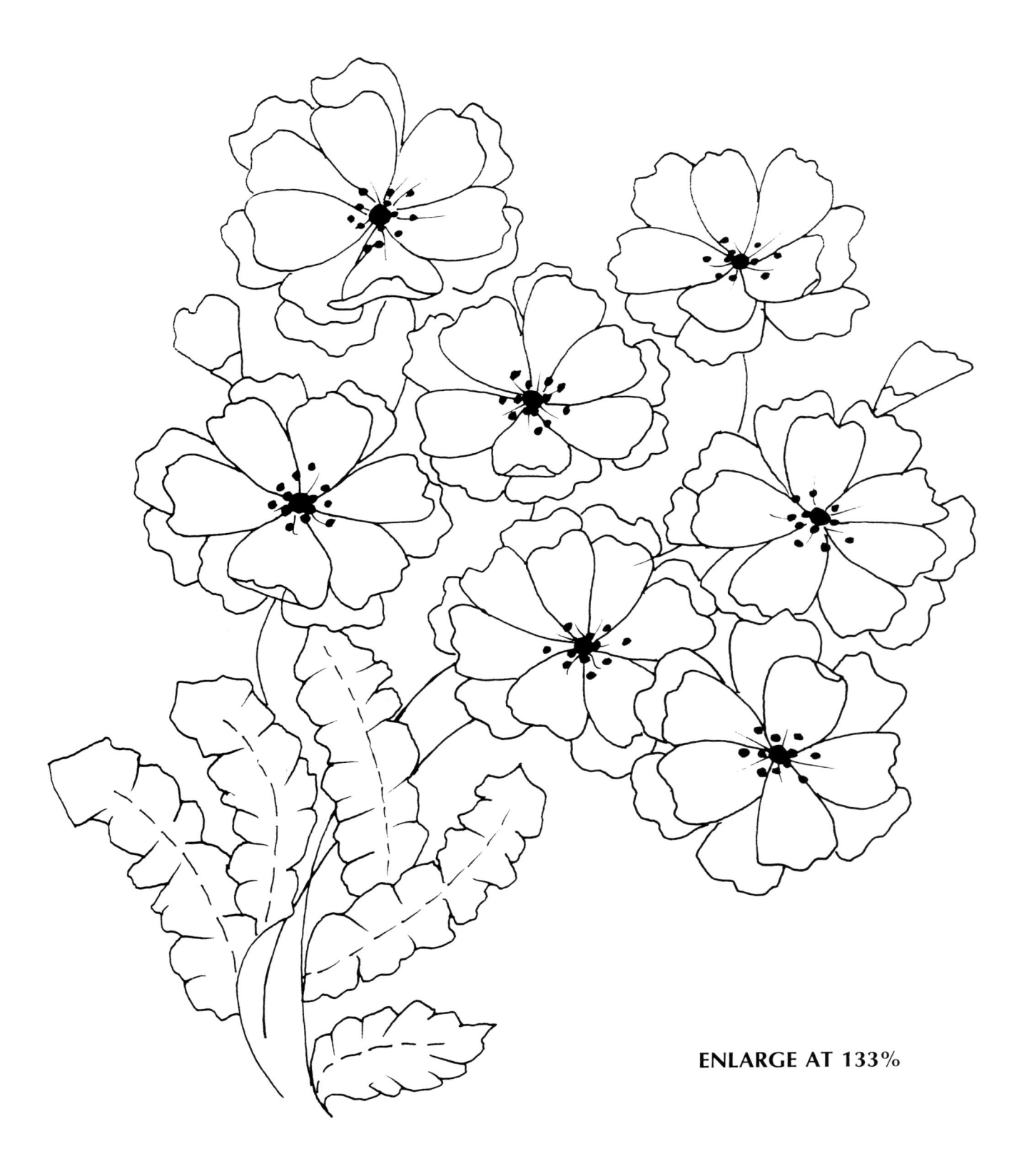

ENLARGE AT 133%

Anemones in taffeta ribbon

Anemones

Frame 32 cm (12½") wooden embroidery hoop
Fabric Cream linen or other suitable fabric (wool-look polyester curtain fabric was used for this) cut at least 6 cm (2¼") larger all around than frame
White lawn the same size for lining
Ribbon 23 mm (1") firm taffeta ribbon in pink, mauve, violet and apple green
20 mm beige satin ribbon for binding hoop
Beads Tiny black beads and a few larger black beads for centres

Trace enlarged design onto fabric. Flowers are best not traced onto fabric, marking in only the centres.

Make flowers first. For each flower cut ribbon into six 4 cm (1½") lengths and six 3.5 mm (1¼") lengths. Trim one end of each petal into a wavy shape. String the six longer pieces onto matching sewing cotton, using running stitches 3 mm (⅛") in from the straight ends. Gather in and stitch ends together to form a circle. Do the same with the six shorter pieces, then sew the second circle down onto the first. Make seven flowers as shown and sew in place.

For each bud use a 3 cm (1¼") length of ribbon, trimmed to a wavy shape at one end, to form a cone and hold at base with a couple of stitches. Trim one end of a short piece of green ribbon into points, wind around lower part of cone and stitch in place. Tuck partly under flowers.

Make stems by laying two lengths of stranded cotton in place on the design and oversewing with couching stitch at 5 mm (¼") intervals with two strands of the same cotton. Take green ribbon, fold corners under neatly to form a point at the tip of the leaf, and secure with a couple of stitches. Take needle through to right side of leaf, place leaf in position on work and take needle through to back of work. Making small folds and gathers with backstitches, sew the centre vein down to form ruffled leaves. Where the leaves meet the stems, tuck ends under and sew down.

Sew a large black bead in the centre of each flower and surround randomly with tiny black beads.

Tighten material in frame, tighten screw, pad back and finish as shown on page 12. Remove embroidery from outer hoop and bind the frame with 20 mm (¾") beige satin ribbon, using craft glue to secure the ends. Return embroidery to hoop, tighten screw well and cover with bow. Attach felt backing with craft glue around edge.

Pattern appears on page 19.

Multi-petalled chrysanthemums in glowing autumn tones

Bowl of chrysanthemums

Frame 32 cm (12½") wooden embroidery hoop
Fabric Dark green slub polyester cut at least 6 cm (2¼") larger all around than hoop
White lawn the same size for lining
Dark green sheer fabric (georgette used here) the same size
Gold crinkled polyester 10 cm (4") in diameter cut across bottom to form base of vase
Ribbon 20 mm (¾") firm taffeta ribbon in yellow, orange, red and dark green
Sewing cotton Matching colours
Beads Small yellow, orange and red beads

First enlarge design and work from this.

Make three flowers in each colour. Cut ribbon for each flower into:
eight 4 cm (1½") lengths
ten 3.5 cm (1¼") lengths
four 2.5 cm (1") lengths
Each flower will take almost a metre (yard).

Take the eight longest pieces first and cut three quarters of the way up with scissors to form four points. See diagram. Stitch running stitches along the blunt ends until the eight pieces are all strung on matching sewing cotton. Gather in fairly tightly and stitch ends together to form circle. Follow the same procedure with the 3.5 cm (1¼") lengths and sew this second circle down to the centre of the first. Repeat with the shortest lengths and sew down. Put the completed flowers away carefully.

Cut left-over ribbon into a number of pointed 'petals' and lay flat. These will be used as filler petals behind the main flowers.

Place the polyester and lawn together and position in frame for a short time to make a circular crease in the fabric. Remove and mark with pencil at top, bottom and sides about 3 cm (1¼") outside the crease.

Lay gold vase piece in position, towards the bottom and a little to the left of centre. Keep in place with a few tiny stitches at top where they will not show. Position filler petals around area where flowers are to go. Lay flowers in position, ensuring that the bases of the filler petals and the top of the vase will be covered by flowers. Secure bases of filler petals with a few tiny stitches to keep in place. Remove flowers and carefully lay sheer green fabric over the work.

When you are sure that everything is in correct position place work carefully over inner hoop. Check again before putting outer hoop in position and tightening screw.

Work a running stitch around vase with two strands of gold stranded cotton and form base with two rows of chain stitch. Use the same gold cotton to work running stitch around the gold petals, red for the red petals and orange for the others. Arrange flowers and stitch to work through the centres. Sew a few matching beads in centres.

Make leaves by folding ends of green ribbon to form a point, catching with a stitch, and then, with running stitches up the centre, gather in and form small pleats with an occasional backstitch. Place leaves in suitable positions, tucked under the flowers, and catch down to work in two or three places.

Tighten fabric in frame, tighten screw, pad back and finish as shown on page 12. Loosen screw and remove embroidery from outer frame. Bind outer frame with dark green ribbon, using craft glue to secure ends. Return embroidery to hoop, tighten screw well and cover with bow. Attach felt backing with craft glue around edge.

Pattern appears on next page.

Bowl of chrysanthemums (page 23)

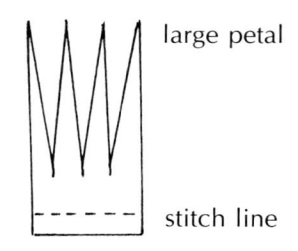

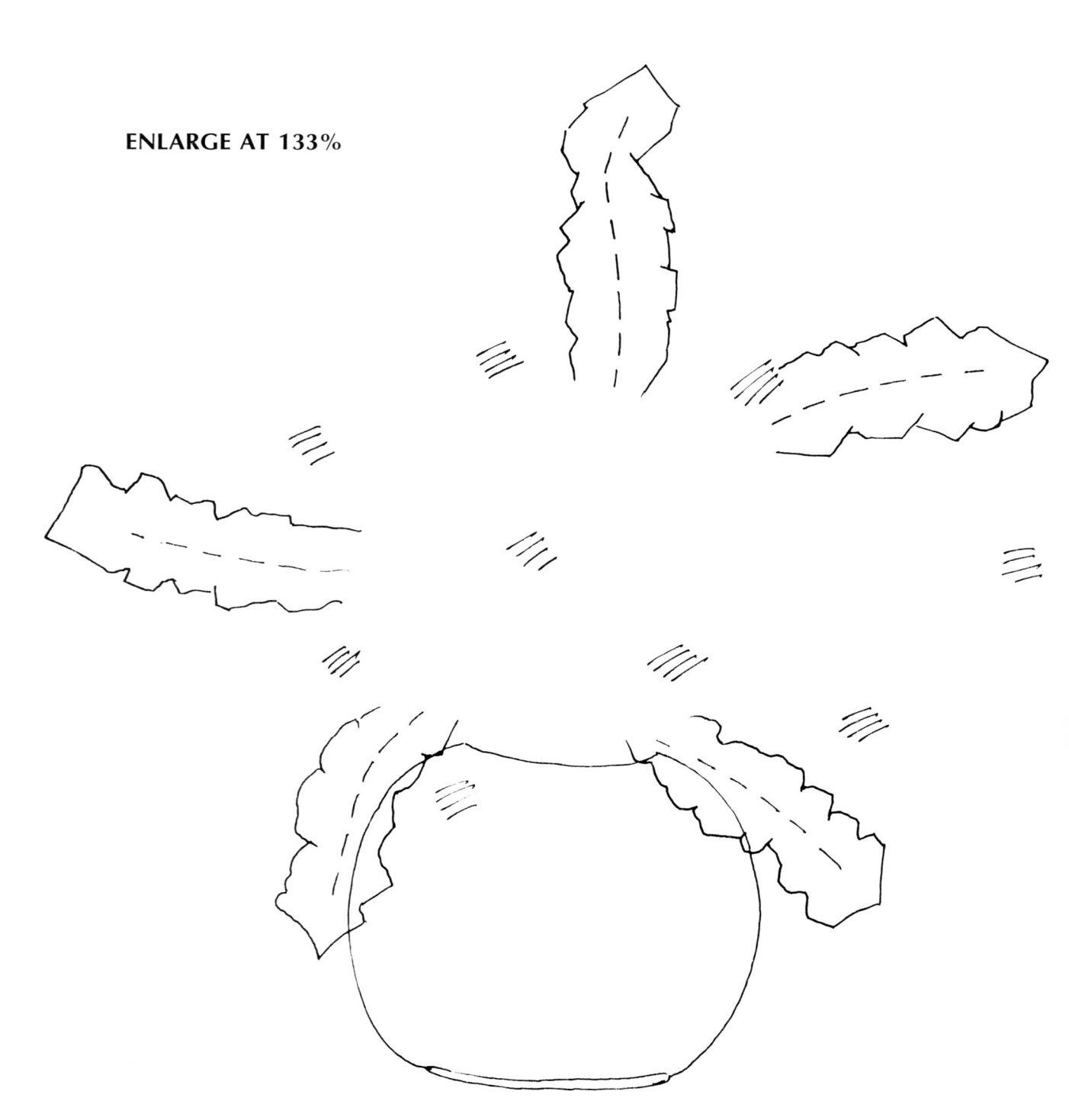

large petal

stitch line

ENLARGE AT 133%

Climbing roses (page 27)

ENLARGE AT 133%

Climbing roses festoon a ribbon trellis. See detail opposite.

26

Climbing roses

Frame   26.5 cm (10½") wooden embroidery hoop
Fabric   Cream linen cut at least 6 cm (2¼") larger all around than hoop
  White lawn the same size for lining
Ribbon   15 mm (⅝") beige satin
  25 mm (1") nylon taffeta in three different pinks
  15 mm (⅝") sheer in white and light and dark pink
  20 mm (¾") green satin
Beads   Small pink, green and a few pearl beads
Fusible web
Glad Bake paper

First enlarge design on page 25 and work from this.

Lay linen and lawn together and place in hoop for a short time to crease the fabric. Remove and make pencil marks at top, bottom and sides about 3 cm (1¼") outside circle.

Pin traced design in position on the circle, slip graphite paper, shiny side down, underneath tracing and go over with ballpoint pen. It is better not to trace the flowers—simply mark in the *centres only*.

Lay lengths of beige ribbon across circle as shown to form lattice, allowing 3 cm (1¼") extra at outer ends, and cut. Remove the ribbon and bond to transfer fusing web, laying them down side by side and right side up with Glad Bake underneath and on top to prevent sticking, and iron well. Peel paper off back carefully, keeping flat to prevent creasing, tear apart carefully and trim with scissors. Arrange ribbons in position on work, cover with Glad Bake and iron well.

Cut leaves from green ribbon, place close together on transfer fusing web with Glad Bake under and over and iron well. Keep flat, tear apart and trim with scissors. Place leaves in position, two or three at a time, and bond to work with the iron, again placing Glad Bake over the top to prevent sticking. Around each leaf, and along centre veins, sew tiny green beads using backstitch.

Use light brown stranded cotton and long backstitches for stems. Make a few prickles with single stitches.

Following the colours in the photograph, begin two flowers in each colourway using 15 cm (6") lengths of the pink taffeta ribbons. Join the ends of each piece and then, using running stitch along one edge, draw in and secure with a couple of stitches. Using matching cotton take two or three tiny running stitches from the outer edge towards the centre, gather and secure with a couple of stitches. Repeat four more times, at evenly spaced intervals, so that the circle resembles five petals. Do this with the base layer for all six flowers.

For the upper layer, gather up similar lengths of the sheer ribbons but do not form petals. Place taffeta ribbon flowers in position on work, secure with a couple of stitches and over each one sew a gathered circle of sheer ribbon, varying the colours. Sew a pearl bead in each centre surrounded with pink beads.

Tighten fabric in frame, tighten screw, pad back and finish as shown on page 12. Loosen the screw and remove the embroidery from the outside frame. Bind with beige satin ribbon, using craft glue to secure ends. Return embroidery to hoop, tighten screw well and cover with bow. Attach felt backing with craft glue around edge.

Apple blossom hibiscus in wire-edged taffeta ribbon

Apple blossom hibiscus

Frame 52 cm × 32 cm (20½" × 12½") oval wooden embroidery hoop
Fabric Dark green slub polyester (or similar) cut at least 6 cm (2¼") larger all around than frame White lawn the same size for lining
Ribbon 23 mm (1") pink wire-edged taffeta ribbon
23 mm (1") green satin ribbon
Beads Tiny cream and green
Tubular pink braid
Stranded cotton Green to tone with satin ribbon
Matching sewing cottons
Glad Bake paper

Lay polyester and lawn together and place in frame for a short time to crease fabric. Remove and mark with pencil at top, bottom and sides about 6 cm (2¼") outside oval crease. Trace design onto fabric, using white graphite paper, and taking care to place it in the correct position. Flowers are better not traced onto fabric—mark in the *centres only*.

Lay three lengths of stranded cotton along main stemlines and oversew, using couching stitch at 5 mm (3/16") intervals with two strands of the same cotton. For minor stems use single lengths of stranded cotton and large backstitches.

Cut green satin ribbon into 4 cm (1½") lengths and trim to leaf shapes. Bond to transfer fusing web, then bond to design after first removing work from frame. Use the Glad Bake paper method described on page 27. Iron leaves on well and return to frame. Sew green beads around edges at 5 mm (3/16") intervals with green sewing cotton, using backstitch.

To make flowers cut pink wired ribbon into 5 cm (2") lengths and trim one end to a rounded shape. String five petals on matching sewing cotton using running stitches 3 mm (1/8") in from the straight end. Gather in tightly and stitch together so that petals stand up and can be bent back. Keeping flowers in this position sew in place. Pistil is made from a 4 cm (1½") piece of tubular pink braid with 5 cm (2") of fine wire, such as a strand of picture wire, passed down through the centre and out the other end. Bend end back up beside braid. Trim other end of wire level with braid.

Make a large knot on the end of a length of matching pink sewing cotton and pass needle down though top of pistil. Bring needle out of side of braid about 5 mm (3/16") down and make a backstitch or two, leaving the knot showing at top of braid. Sew about eight cream beads around pistil, following diagram and photograph, taking needle through braid and using backstitches. With a stiletto make a hole down centre of flower and through the background fabric to back of work. Pass lower end of pistil through the hole to the back, adjust the bend in the wire and sew down.

Tighten work in frame, tighten screw, pad back and finish as shown on page 12. Loosen screw and remove embroidery from outer frame. Bind outer frame with green satin ribbon, using craft glue to secure ends. Return embroidery to hoop, tighten screw well and cover with bow. Attach felt backing with craft glue around edge.

Detail of flowers

top of pattern

join

Apple blossom hibiscus
(page 29)

30

join

ENLARGE AT 133%

31

Red roses in crinkle polyester

Red roses

Frame   52 cm × 32 cm (20½ × 12½") wooden embroidery frame
Fabric   Cream linen cut at least 6 cm (2¼") larger all around than hoop
   White lawn the same size for lining
   Crinkle polyester in bright red, dark red and dark green
Beads   Tiny red and gold beads
Ribbon   Dark green 23 mm (1") taffeta to bind hoop
Stranded cotton   Dark green
Matching sewing cottons

First enlarge design to work from.

Lay linen and lawn together and place in frame for a short time to form a crease. Remove and mark with pencil on top, bottom and sides about 3 cm (1¼") outside oval crease. Trace enlarged design in position on fabric. Return fabric to frame and tighten screw.

Cut out five 10 cm (4") circles of bright red polyester and five 10 cm (4") circles of dark red. Using matching sewing cotton sew running stitches 3 mm (⅛") in around the edge of each circle. Gather in a little and finish off with a couple of stitches. Make about five long stitches on the wrong side inside each circle and draw in loosely to give the appearance of a rose. Pin three or four flowers in position on design and catch edges here and there with tiny stitches in matching sewing cotton. Let some flowers overlap others a little. Sew a few red and gold beads into their centres as shown in the photographs. Continue until all flowers are in position.

Cut out 18 large leaves and 20 smaller leaves from the dark green fabric following the pattern shapes. Place two pieces together face to face and machine or sew running stitch around the edges, leaving about 10 mm (⅜") open at top to turn leaves out to the right side. Turn raw edges in and

Detail of red roses showing beading

top of pattern

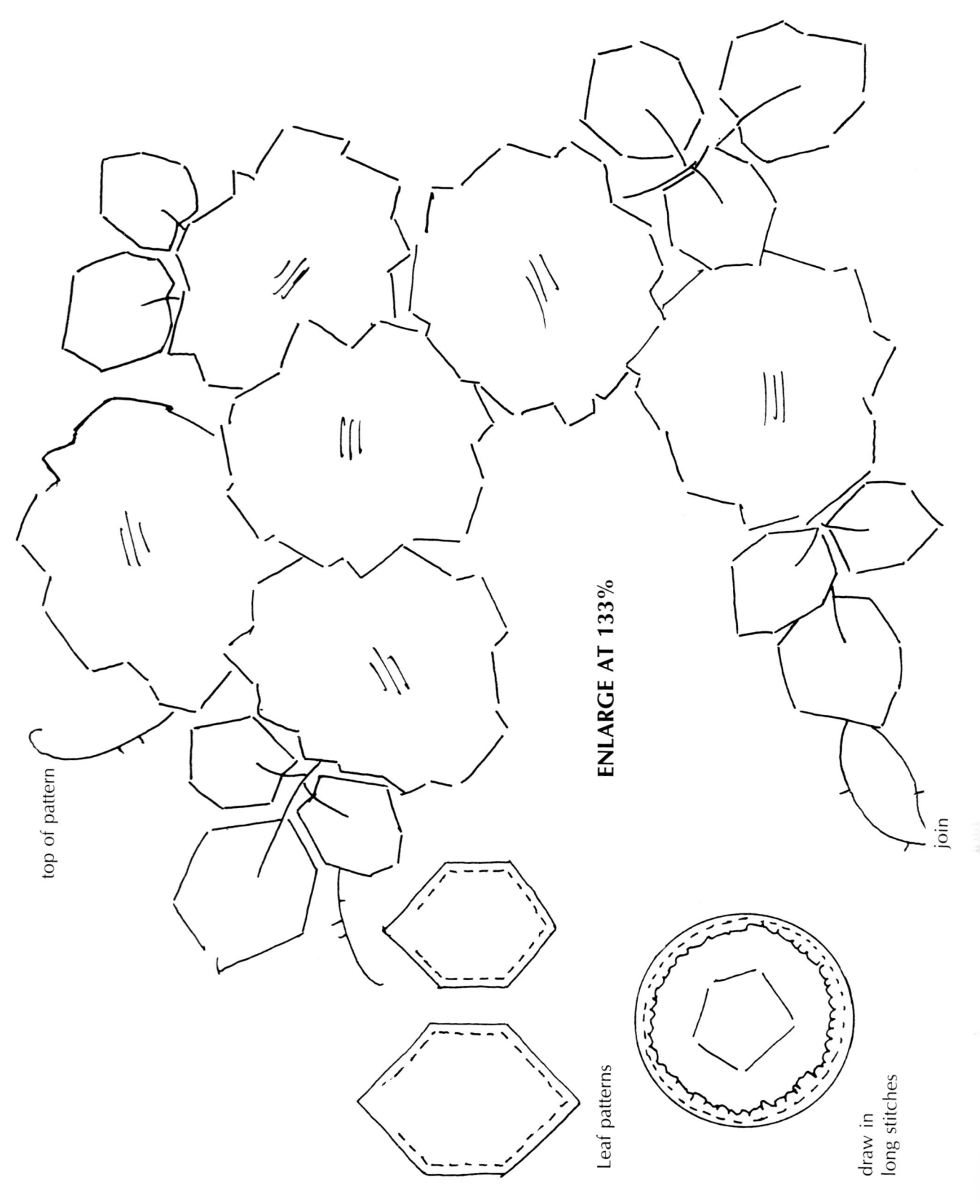

ENLARGE AT 133%

join

Leaf patterns

draw in
long stitches

34

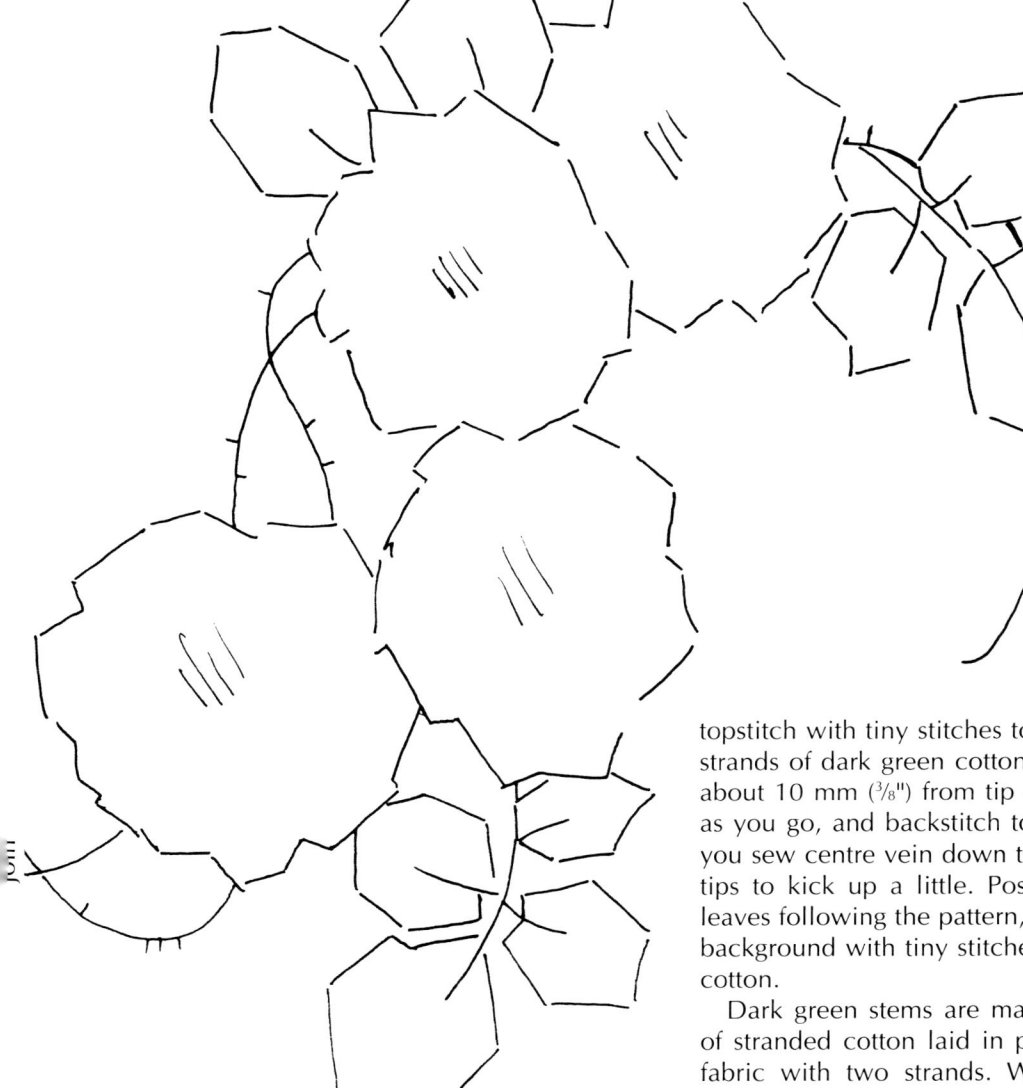

topstitch with tiny stitches to finish off. Using two strands of dark green cotton start a running stitch about 10 mm (3/8") from tip of leaf. Gather a little as you go, and backstitch to form more pleats as you sew centre vein down to fabric, allowing leaf tips to kick up a little. Position large and small leaves following the pattern, catching down to the background with tiny stitches in matching sewing cotton.

Dark green stems are made with three lengths of stranded cotton laid in place and whipped to fabric with two strands. Work the ends of the stems in under flowers and leaves.

Tighten material in frame, tighten screw, pad back and finish as shown on page 12. Remove embroidery from outside hoop and bind with 23 mm (1") dark green taffeta ribbon, using craft glue to secure ends. Return embroidery to hoop, tighten screw and cover with green ribbon bow. Attach felt backing with craft glue around edge.

Pink roses in crinkle polyester

Pink roses

This design is a smaller circular variation of the preceding 'Red roses' design. Follow those instructions for making up.

Frame   21 cm (8¼") wooden embroidery hoop
Fabric   Cream linen cut at least 6 cm (2¼") larger all around than hoop
   White lawn the same size for lining
   Crinkle polyester in pink and dark green
Beads   Tiny pink and gold beads
Ribbon   Light green 23 mm (1") taffeta to bind hoop
Stranded cotton   Dark green and light green
Matching sewing cottons

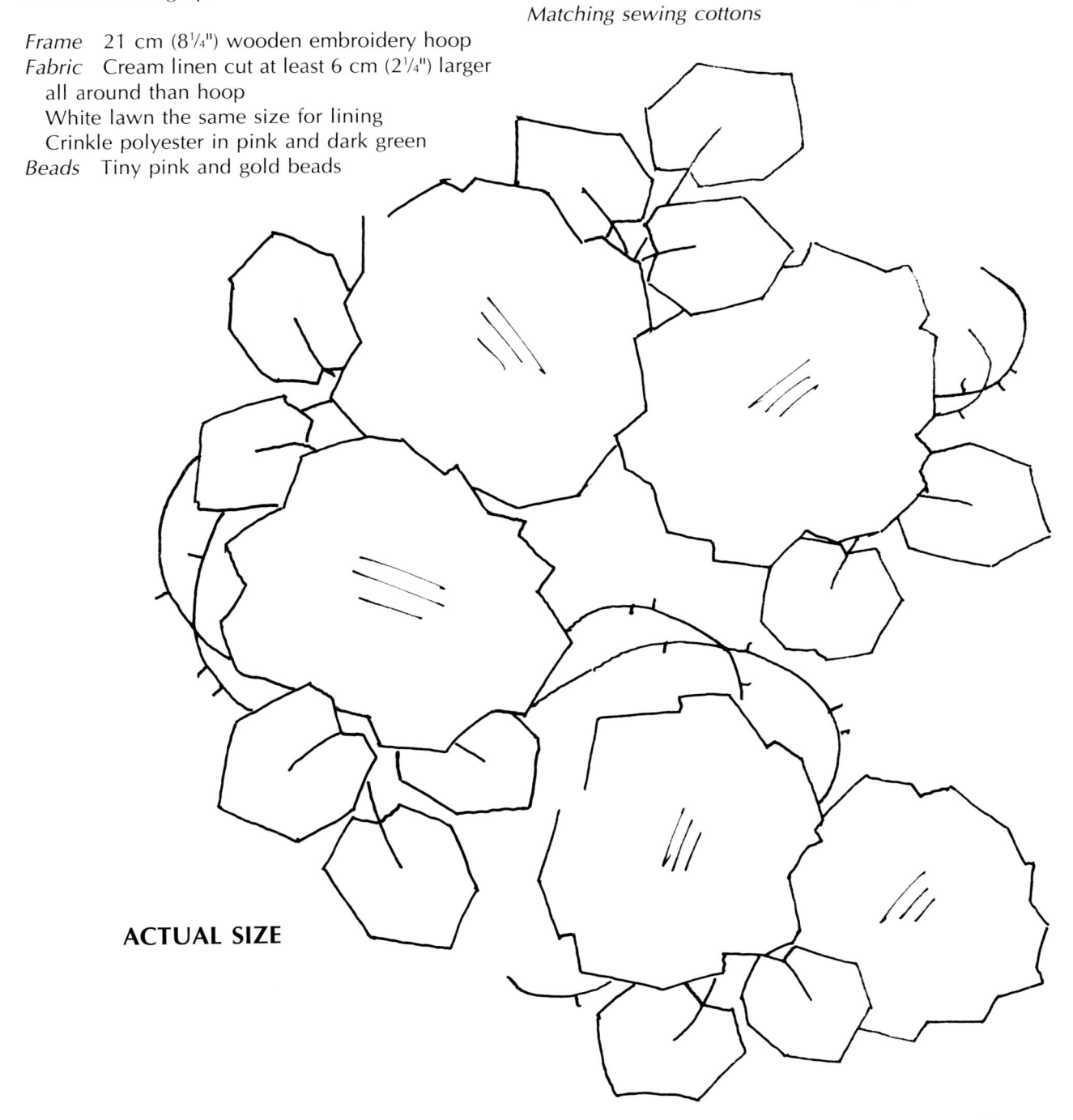

ACTUAL SIZE

Spectacular chrysanthemums in wire-edged taffeta ribbon

Pink and purple chrysanthemums

Frame 32 cm (12½") wooden embroidery hoop
Fabric Cream linen cut at least 6 cm (2¼") larger all around than frame
White lawn the same size for lining
Ribbon 23 mm (1") wire-edged taffeta in pink, purple and violet
3 mm black satin
Scraps of black taffeta or black ribbon for leaves
Beads Small gold
Matching sewing cottons
Transfer fusing web
Glad Bake paper

Make three flowers in each colour first. Cut ribbon for each flower into:
 ten 4 cm (1½") lengths
 eight 3.5 cm (1¼") lengths
 four 2.5 cm (1") lengths
 Each flower will take almost a metre.

Take longest pieces first and cut three quarters of the way up with scissors to form four points, as shown in the diagram. Using running stitches along the blunt ends, string ten long pieces together on a length of matching sewing cotton. Gather in fairly tightly and stitch ends together to form circle. Do the same with the 3.5 cm (1¼") lengths, then sew second circle down to centre of first. Repeat with the shortest lengths and sew down.

Lay linen and lawn together and place in frame for a short time to make a crease. Remove and mark with pencil at top, bottom and sides about 3 cm (1¼") outside circle. Pin traced design in position and slip graphite paper underneath. Trace design on, marking only centres of flowers, and making sure stems will be running straight up and down with weave of fabric. Return fabric to frame.

Bring 3 mm black ribbon through from back, leaving about 1 cm (3/8") behind work. Pin in place and with tiny stitches about 1 cm (3/8") apart, sew ribbon in place close to the edge on each side. Take ends through to back and catch down.

Cut leaves from black ribbon, place close together on transfer fusing web with Glad Bake paper under and over and iron well. Keeping flat, tear apart and trim with scissors. Take work out of frame again, place leaves in position and with a small piece of Glad Bake over each one, iron on one at a time to bond. Place back in frame.

Lay flowers in position and stitch to work through centres. Sew gold beads in centres and over base of petals to keep flowers open.

Tighten fabric in frame, tighten screw, pad back and finish as shown on page 12. Attach felt backing with craft glue, and cover screw with a ribbon bow to match the flowers.

Pattern appears on next page.

Pink and purple chrysanthemums (page 39)

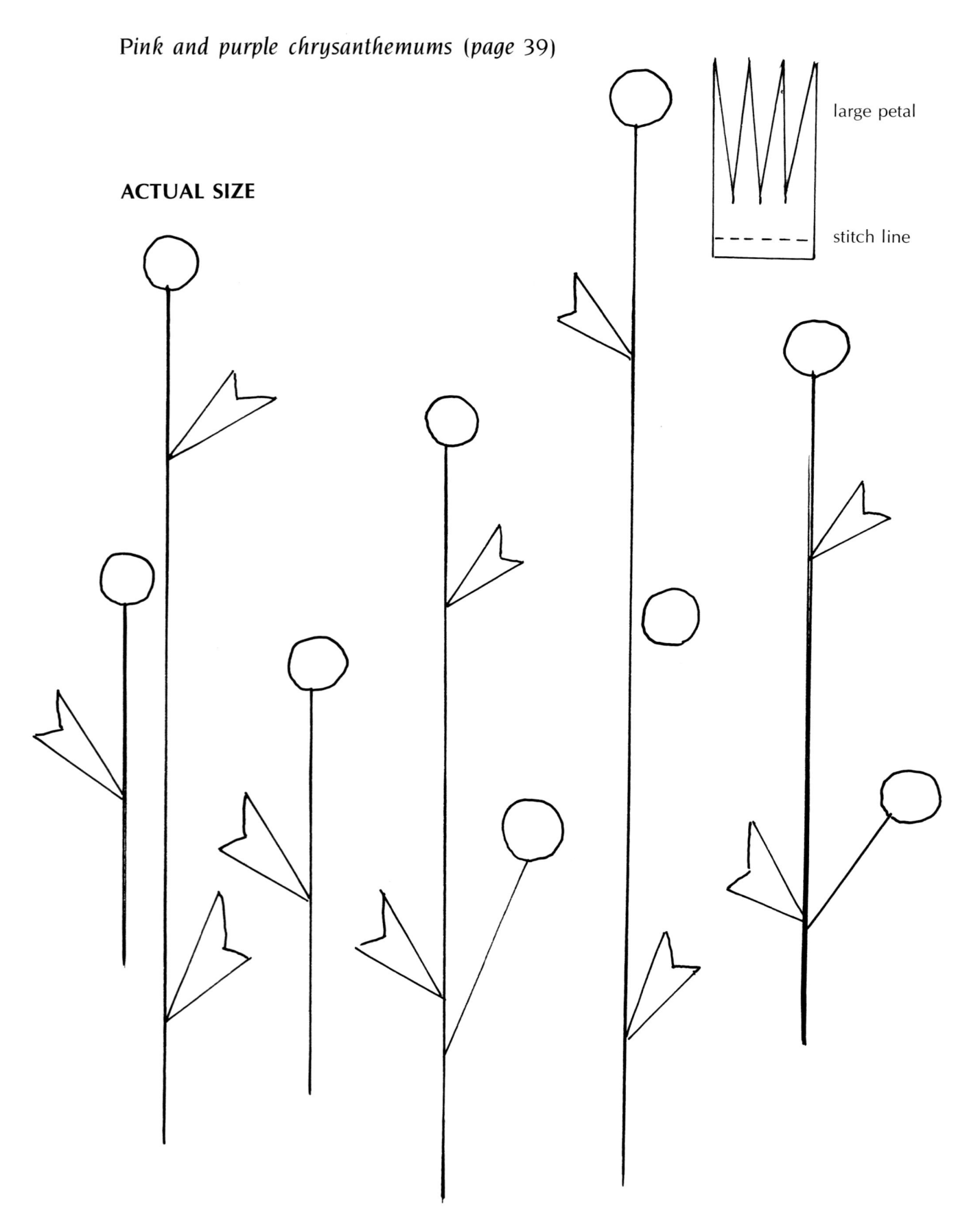

ACTUAL SIZE

large petal

stitch line

40

Large rose plaque (page 42)

ACTUAL SIZE

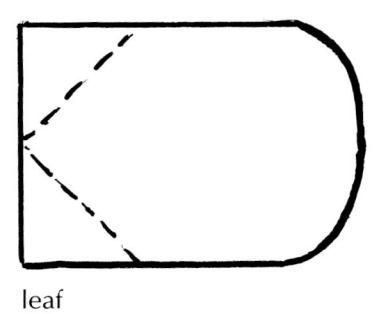

leaf

Large rose plaque

Particle board   80 cm × 54 cm (31½" × 21¼")
Plastic sheet foam   3–4 mm (⅛") thick, and 7 cm (2¾") larger all around than board
Background fabric   Suede-coated polyester and cotton curtain material in soft colours and fairly plain designs, 7 cm (2¾") larger all around than board
Fabric for flowers and leaves   Plain suede-coated curtain material—pink, blue, beige and light green in this case—to match background
Beads   For centres and background outlines (optional) in toning colours and clear
Felt backing
Matching sewing cottons

For each flower, trace outlines of each of the three flower pieces on page 41 on back of plain material and cut out inside the lines to avoid black edges. Use running stitches around centre hole of each piece and gather in.

Place pieces one on top of another as in the photographs and sew together in centre. Tiny clear beads may be attached to flowers to resemble raindrops. Group flowers together in desired position on background, sew in place and add beads in centres.

Cut out leaves from pattern, turn corners of straight end in towards centre and fix in place with tiny stitches at back. Run a few stitches down centre from rounded end in sewing cotton or two strands of stranded cotton, taking one or two tucks. Tuck leaves partly under flowers and sew in place with tiny stitches in one or two places down centre. Matching tiny beads can be used to outline background design. Use backstitch and keep about 5 mm (¼") apart.

To finish, cover board with plastic sheet foam and staple edges to back. Cover with finished embroidery and staple also. Staple cord to each side to hang.

Simple but effective, soft-coloured roses in suede-coated curtain fabric

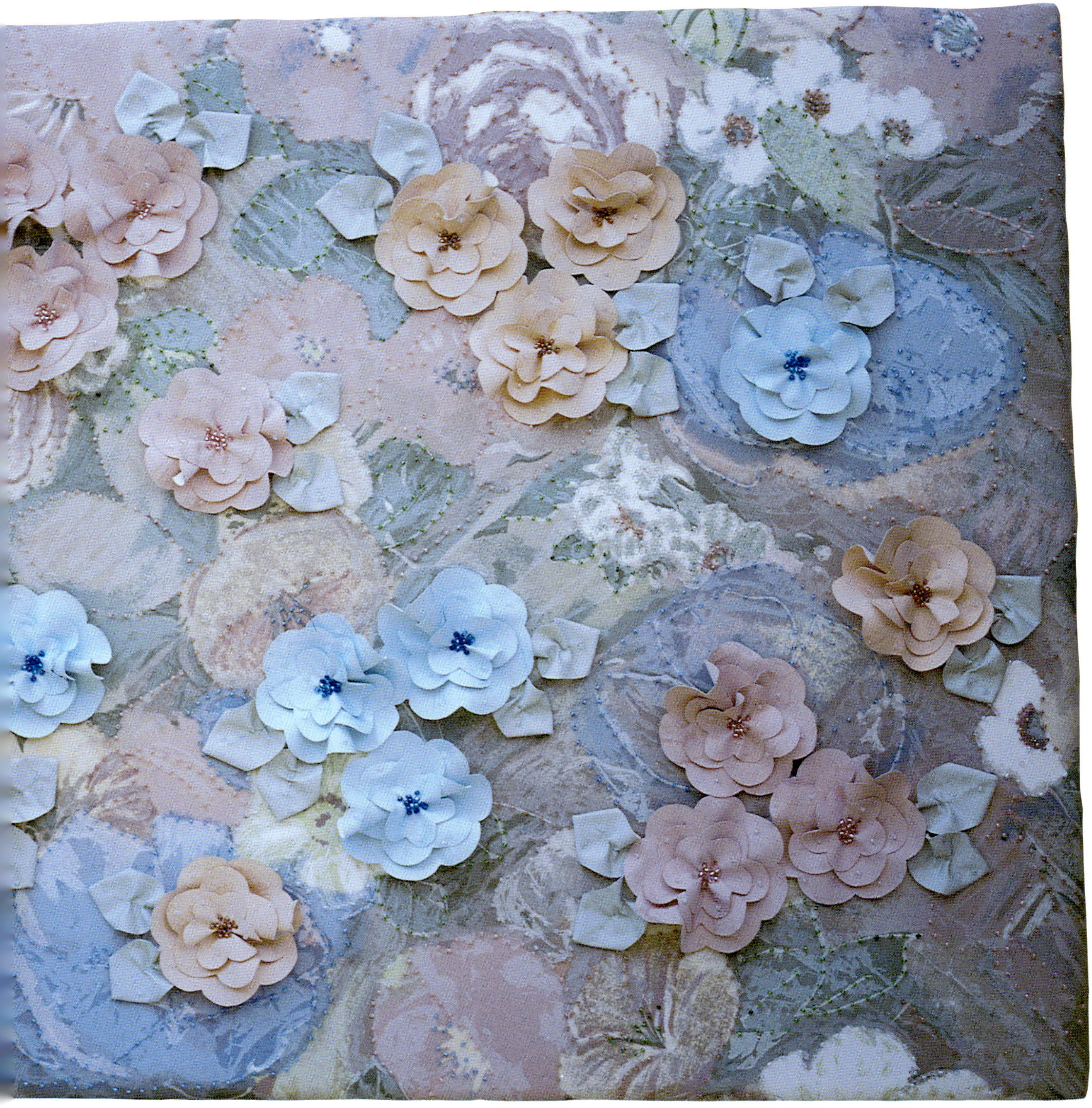

Cheerful sunflowers in three shades of yellow satin ribbon

Sunflowers

Frame 32 cm × 52 cm (12½ × 20½") oval wooden embroidery frame
Fabric Cream linen or other suitable material (wool-look polyester curtain fabric was used here) cut at least 6 cm (2¼") larger all around than frame
White lawn the same size for lining
Ribbon 17 mm (⅝") satin in three yellows
23 mm (1") satin in green
6 mm (¼") satin in green
Wool Various shades of brown
Matching sewing cottons

Enlarge pattern before you start to work.

Place two fabrics together in frame and screw tight. Leave for a short time. Loosen screw and take material out of frame. There will be a crease the shape of the frame. Make pencil marks at top, bottom and sides 3 cm (1¼") outside oval. This is to facilitate tracing and returning work to correct position.

Trace design. If you are using a thick fabric, make holes in paper with a stiletto at base and tip of each petal and at top and bottom of leaves and stems. Ensuring that stems will be running straight up and down with weave of fabric, place design over fabric in correct position and use a pencil to mark through each hole.

Return fabric to frame, check direction of stems again, and tighten screw. Start with the lightest or dullest yellow ribbon for petals which are mostly underneath others. Using a stiletto to make a hole, bring ribbon up at edge of centre, leaving about 2 cm (¾") at back. Take through to back at tip of petal and bring up again at centre edge. If you wish to follow the colours as seen in the picture then do so, otherwise work this way: Continue randomly with the light ribbon, mostly on right-hand side of each flower, leaving a little space between petals. Take the medium yellow and create petals along left-hand (lighter) side of flowers, adding some in between the pale ones on the right. The deepest yellow goes mainly on the left-hand side in between the medium yellow petals, with just a few on the right side.

Fill the centres with French knots in the brown wools, varying the colours as in the photographs.

Pin stems in postion using 6 mm (¼") green ribbon and allowing extra 2–3 cm (1") to tuck under frame at bottom of work when finishing off. Catch down at intervals with tiny stitches in matching sewing cotton.

Turn tips of 23 mm (1") green ribbon under as shown and fix with a couple of stitches. Take needle through to right side of leaf in centre, place leaf in position on work and take needle through to back. Making small folds and gathers with backstitches, sew the centre vein down to form leaves which tuck under the flowers.

Tighten fabric in frame, tighten screw, pad back and finish as shown on page 12. Loosen screw and remove embroidery from outside frame. Bind the frame with 23 mm (1") green satin ribbon, using craft glue to secure ends. Return embroidery to hoop, tighten screw well and cover with bow. Attach felt backing with craft glue around edge.

Note variations of tone in French knot centres

Sunflowers

46

join

ENLARGE AT 133%

Pink, white and blue flowers

Cardboard Strong cardboard 40 cm × 24 cm (16" × 9½"). Use two sheets if necessary.
Background fabric Suede-coated polyester and cotton curtain fabric cut 5 cm (2") larger all around than required size
Fabric for flowers and leaves Plain suede-coated curtain material to suit background colours
Ribbon 3 mm green satin for stems
Beads Small black, yellow and green for centres
Strong crochet cotton (or thin string) to lace back
Matching sewing cottons
Felt backing

Enlarge pattern before tracing design onto background, marking only stems, centres of flowers and leaves. For white flowers trace and cut out 40 white petals, cutting inside the lines to avoid black edges. For each flower take five petals and string them together with running stitches 3 mm (⅛") in from the straight edges. Gather in fairly tightly and stitch together so that petals stand up a little. Sew in position on design. Cut out circles of green fabric for centres and sew in place with beads.

The smaller pink and blue flowers are made by cutting 3 cm (1¼") squares: 11 in the blue fabric and 7 in the pink. Fold each one into four and cut out centre, 3 mm (⅛") in from folded corner. Cut off the corners and round them. With a running stitch, gather centre in, sew in position on work and add black bead for centre.

Cut out leaves, gather straight edge of each one with running stitch and sew into position on design.

Pin stems in position and sew down with tiny stitches in matching cotton where necessary.

Cut cardboard to size with a Stanley knife. Lay embroidery over cardboard and, using bodkin or very thick needle and crochet cotton or thin string, lace from side to side and end to end firmly, as shown in the picture on page 13. Felt backing can be applied with craft glue.

Simple flower shapes in suede-coated curtain fabric

Pink, white and blue flowers

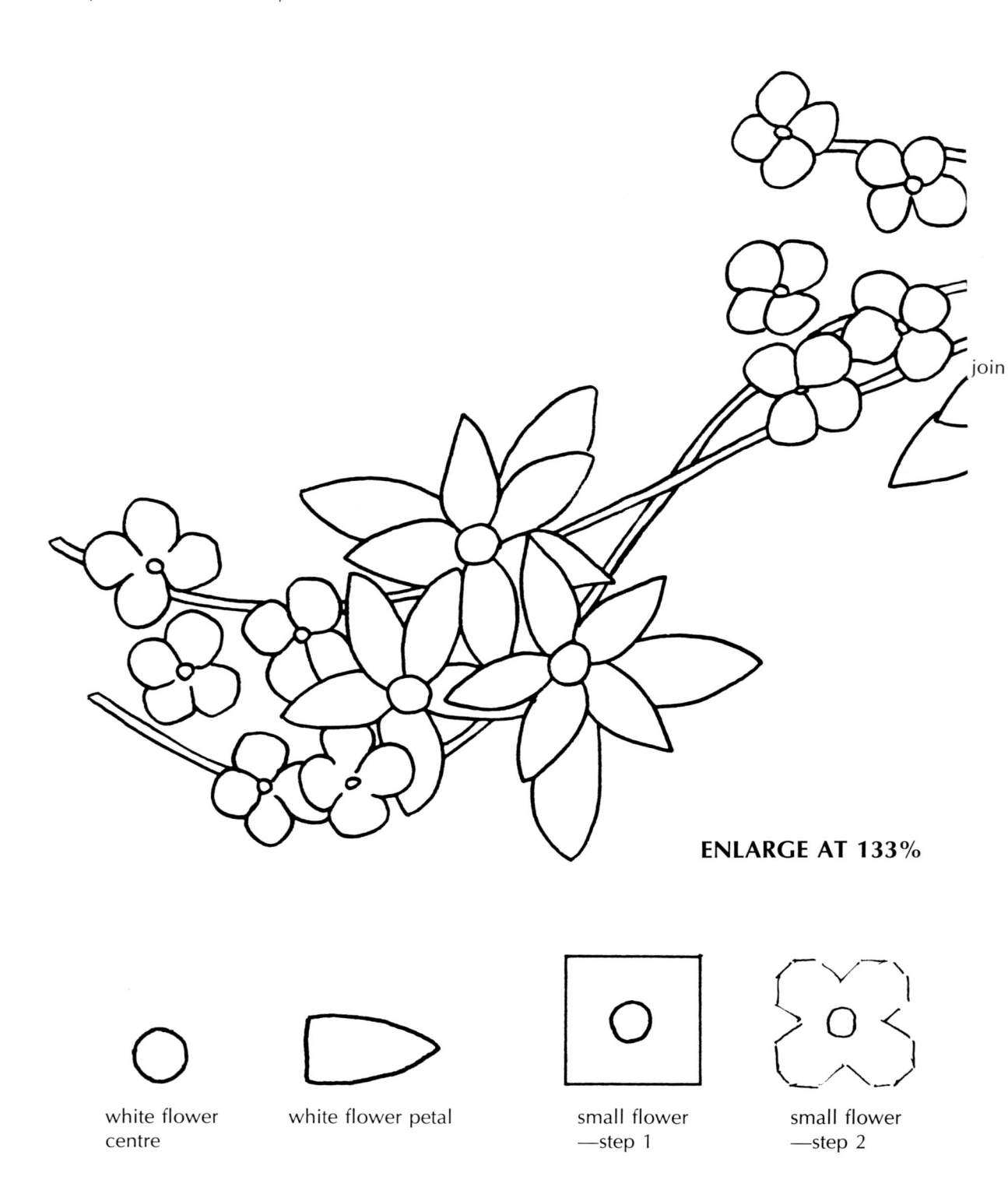

join

ENLARGE AT 133%

white flower centre

white flower petal

small flower —step 1

small flower —step 2

join

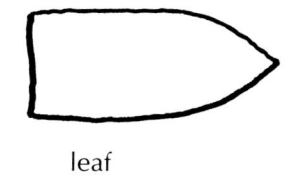

leaf

51

Daisy shapes make a strong statement

Daisy plaque

Cardboard   Strong cardboard 40 cm × 24 cm (16" × 9½"). Use two sheets if necessary.

Background fabric   Suede-coated polyester and cotton curtain fabric 5 cm (2") larger all around than required size

Fabric for flowers and leaves   Plain suede-coated curtain fabric—light and dark pink, cream and green used here—to suit background

Ribbon   3 mm green satin for stems

Beads   Small gold beads for centres

Matching sewing cottons

Crochet cotton   to lace back

Felt backing

Trace enlarged design onto background, marking only stems, centres of flowers and leaves. Each flower is made with about 22 petals. To make each one cut a strip of fabric 20 cm × 27 mm (8" × 1⅛"). Mark dots along each side at 9 mm (⅜") intervals. Cut across from dot on one side to 4 mm (³⁄₁₆") from dot on other side along strip and then cut corners, as shown on diagram. With a running stitch along joined edge gather fairly tightly and overlap, forming a double row of petals. Sew in position on design.

Make the bud with three or four petals, and the profile flower with eight or nine.

To make leaves, trace 14 shapes onto back of green material and cut out inside outline to avoid black edges. With a double thread of matching sewing cotton sew a running stitch starting about 15 mm (⅝") from tip to base, and gather slightly. Stitch in place under flowers as shown. Allowing some slack, fix with a stitch at other end of running stitches.

Pin ribbon stems in position and, with tiny stitches, where necessary fix in place.

Cut green circles for centres of flowers and sew in place with three beads.

Cut out calyx for profile flowers and sew down with a few tiny stitches.

Cut cardboard to size with Stanley knife. Lay embroidery over cardboard and, using bodkin or very thick needle and crochet cotton or thin string, lace from side to side and end to end firmly as shown in picture on page 13. Felt backing can be applied with craft glue.

Detail of daisy plaque

Daisy plaque

ENLARGE AT 133%

petals

bud calyx

profile flower calyx

join

54

join

centres

leaf

55

Folded roses used for three-dimensional effect in a small embroidery

Yellow folded roses with violets

Frame 17 cm (6¾") round plastic
Fabric Fine linen cut at least 4 cm (1½") larger all around than frame
White lawn the same size
Ribbon 7 mm satin in golden yellow and chartreuse
3 mm satin in violet, light brown and pale blue
Stranded cotton Chartreuse, light brown and orange
Matching sewing cottons

Lay linen and lawn together and place in frame.

Make the folded roses first as shown on page 11, and sew in place on design. Use straight stitches for violets and brown leaves.

Backstitch stems in two strands of chartreuse and light brown stranded cotton and then work French knots in blue ribbon.

Work violet centres using two strands of orange stranded cotton to make tiny French knots.

Tighten fabric in frame and finish back.

ACTUAL SIZE

Pink single roses

Frame   9 cm (3½") circular plastic
Fabric   White silk cut at least 3 cm (1¼") larger all around than frame
   White lawn the same size as lining
Ribbon   7 mm silk in pink
   3 mm silk in deep pink and grey
Beads   A few gold and pink, very small
Stranded cotton   Orange and grey

Lay silk and lawn together and place in frame. Apply traced design using graphite paper shiny side down. Work pink single roses with loose straight stitches. Slip a wooden skewer under ribbon near outer edge of each petal while pulling the ribbon through to the back. This keeps the petal wide at outer edge.

For the small flowers and buds work loose straight stitches in the deep pink ribbon and sew a tiny pink bead in each centre. With a single thread of orange stranded cotton work tiny stitches on top of the inner part of each petal to suggest stamens and to make petals puffier towards outer edge. Sew a tiny gold bead in each centre.

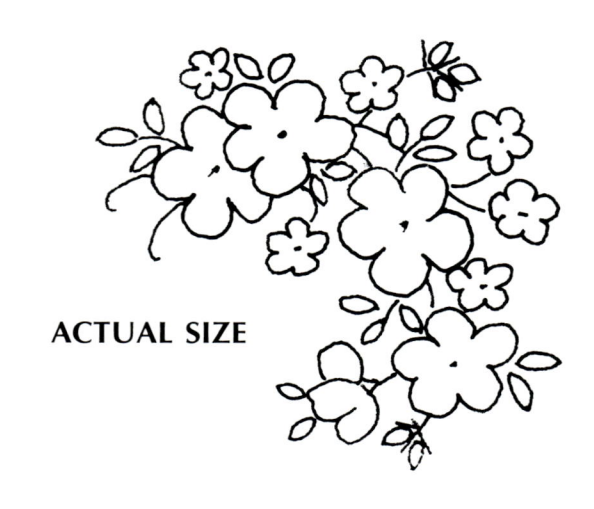

For the leaves use grey silk ribbon and straight stitches. Backstitch stems with two strands of grey cotton.

Tighten fabric in frame and finish back as shown on page 12.

ACTUAL SIZE

Miniature pink single roses

Small mauve ribbon roses

Frame 9 cm (3½") circular plastic
Fabric Pale blue crinkled polyester cut at least 4 cm (1½") larger all around than frame
White lawn the same size as lining
Ribbon 3 mm variegated silk ribbon if obtainable, *or* different shades of soft pinks and mauves or purples
3 mm silk ribbon in white, blue and green
Stranded cotton Yellow, green and pale green
Matching sewing cottons

Lay silk and lawn together and place in frame. Apply traced design using graphite paper shiny side down.

Make the ribbon roses first using fly stitch in a matching cotton as the base and weaving the ribbon over and under the spokes until the cotton is covered.

Tiny white flowers are worked in short, loose straight stitches with a tiny stitch in the centre of each in two strands of yellow stranded cotton.

Place tiny purple rosebuds in position with single straight stitches in purple ribbon and two stitches in green ribbon. Leaves are also formed with single stitches in green ribbon.

Backstitch stems in pale green using a single strand of cotton.

Finish with French knots in blue ribbon.

Tighten material in frame and finish back following the picture on page 12.

ACTUAL SIZE

Miniature folded roses in variegated silk ribbon

Doll's hat with braided ribbon and ribbon roses

Straw doll's hat Obtainable at most craft shops
Lace Gathered with bound edge
Ribbon 4 m of 5 mm (¼") satin ribbon (firm) for braiding
   10 mm firm satin ribbon in three colours for folded roses on hat, 3 m of each colour

Make folded roses as shown on page 11, six in each colour.
   Braid the 5 mm ribbon (see diagram):
1. Fold ribbon in half, right side out, and sew a couple of stitches 8 mm (⅜") in from folded end to form a loop.

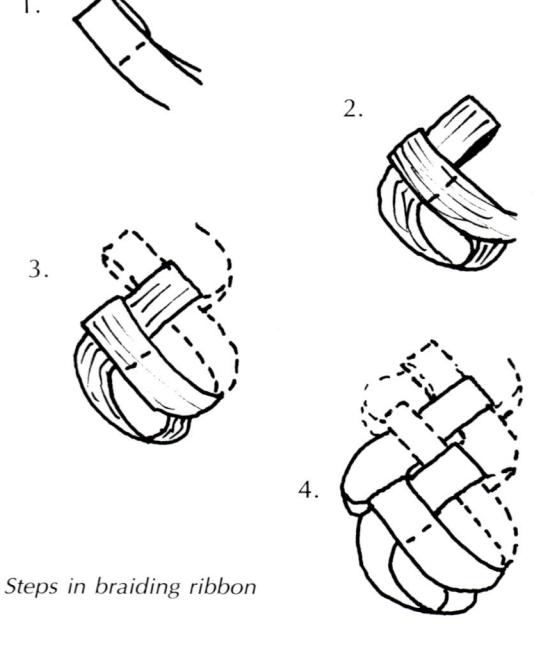

Steps in braiding ribbon

2. Take one piece of next part of ribbon and fold over, right side out and push through loop as shown.
3. Fold other piece over and push through second loop. Tighten as you go.
4. Continue with first one side and then the other until you have the required length.
   With craft glue attach gathered edge of lace to top edge of hat brim and around crown. Glue braid around, overlapping bound edge of lace. Pass end of braid through opposite end and tie a bow to finish off. Arrange roses and glue around crown.

Doll's hat to delight any small girl

Round box with braided ribbon and ribbon roses

Small round woven straw box
Lace Gathered with bound edge
Ribbon 3 m of 5 mm (¼") firm satin ribbon for braiding

7 mm firm satin ribbon in two pinks (2 m of each for folded roses)
Rose leaves 6 artificial rose leaves

Make seven folded roses and braid ribbon as described for preceding design.

Using craft glue, attach two rows of lace to top of box, one facing outwards and the other in, with a space of about 5 mm (¼") in between.

Place braided ribbon between rows of lace and finish with a bow. In the centre glue six leaves and seven folded roses.

Glue a row of lace with ribbon covering the bound edge around side of box.